OUR LADY OF KIBEHO
AND THE ROSARY OF THE SEVEN SORROWS

Coloring Book

**Written by
Betty McMillan**

**Illustrated by
Mary Lou Jacquin**

BALBOA
PRESS
A DIVISION OF HAY HOUSE

Balboa Press books may be ordered through booksellers or by contacting:

Balboa Press
A Division of Hay House
1663 Liberty Drive
Bloomington, IN 47403
www.balboapress.com
1 (877) 407-4847

Because of the dynamic nature of the Internet, any web addresses or links contained in this book may have changed since publication and may no longer be valid. The views expressed in this work are solely those of the author and do not necessarily reflect the views of the publisher, and the publisher hereby disclaims any responsibility for them.

The author of this book does not dispense medical advice or prescribe the use of any technique as a form of treatment for physical, emotional, or medical problems without the advice of a physician, either directly or indirectly. The intent of the author is only to offer information of a general nature to help you in your quest for emotional and spiritual well-being. In the event you use any of the information in this book for yourself, which is your constitutional right, the author and the publisher assume no responsibility for your actions.

Any people depicted in stock imagery provided by Thinkstock are models, and such images are being used for illustrative purposes only.
Certain stock imagery © Thinkstock.

ISBN: 978-1-5043-3782-3 (sc)
ISBN: 978-1-5043-3783-0 (e)

Print information available on the last page.

Balboa Press rev. date: 09/02/2015

DEDICATED TO FOUR MOTHERS

TO MARY LOUISE (CLINGMAN) COSTIGAN,
Whose love for the Blessed Virgin was so great she dedicated her three
children, (Patty Costigan Sevening, Mary Lou Costigan Jacquin, and
Betty Costigan McMillan) to Her. For the first seven years of each of
their lives to honor their Heavenly Mother she dressed them only in
the colors of the Virgin, blue and white. If there was the tiniest bit
of trim, (e.g. a little pink bunny at Easter,) it was carefully removed.
Mary Louise imparted this love of the Virgin to her daughters.

TO ANNE (MARGOLE) McMILLAN,
Who always kept a rosary in her apron pocket.

TO ROSE KANKINDI,
Whose spirituality was a way of life. Her life was a reflection of motherly love
to all she encountered, pupils, neighbors, friends, total strangers, but most
of all to her family. Her motherly love is still reflected today in her daughter,
Immaculee Ilibagiza. Immaculee spends her life spreading this love and
knowledge of Our Lady of Kibeho and the Seven Sorrows Rosary to others.

TO THE BLESSED VIRGIN, THE MOTHER OF GOD
Who is the Mother of the Word and the Mother of the
world, Who cares about our biggest and our smallest needs,
Who is always with us, and brings us to Her Son.

Just before Our Lord, Jesus Christ, died, He gave us the most wonderful gift. He gave us His own mother to be our own mother.

Now, Mother Mary never died. One day, She went to sleep and She was taken up to heaven to be with Her Son, Jesus. She still watches over us and cares for us because we are Her children.

Many years went by since Mary was taken to heaven. When Mother Mary looked down from heaven on all Her children, what She saw made Her sad. Her children were not obeying the commandments of Her Son, Jesus. Her children were not showing love to Him or to one another.

Our Blessed Mother was so sad. She asked Her Son if She could visit earth again to try to help Her children.

When Jesus said, "Yes," Mary went to Rwanda. She visited some teenaged school girls in a small village named Kibeho. At first people did not believe the girls were being visited by the Mother of Jesus.

In time more and more people began to believe in the girls. People
wanted to be there when Mary visited the girls, even if they could
not see Mary themselves. The crowds grew and grew. Soon there
were thousands of people when Mary came to see the girls.

They called the girls visionaries. Mary gave each visionary a different job to do. In a visit to the visionary, Marie Claire, Mary was holding a rosary. Mary asked Marie Claire to teach the world to pray this rosary. Marie Claire said she never saw a rosary quite like the one Mary was holding. A hand came from the crowd and gave Marie Claire a rosary just like the one Mary was holding.

The rosary was different than the one Marie Claire was used to praying. Over the next few visits the Blessed Mother taught Marie Claire how to pray it. Mary told Marie Claire She had given it to the world before, but people stopped praying it. She asked Marie Claire to teach it to the whole world.

Marie Claire wanted to obey the Blessed Mother, but she didn't know what to do. She didn't even have money to take a taxi. How could she spread the rosary to the whole world? Mary told her to give the rosary to her parish priest. Mary said that he would know what to do.

The parish priest sent the rosary to Rome to the head of the whole Catholic Church. The Church checked back in all its historical records. They found that the rosary that Mary gave to Marie Claire was the same exact rosary and words She gave to St. Brigid of Sweden in the thirteenth century.

Marie Claire only knew the language of Rwanda, Kinyarwanda. She did not know Latin, Swedish, or ancient history. That is how the church leaders KNEW the rosary was truly a gift from the Virgin Mary, Our Mother.

The Blessed Virgin told Marie Claire to teach the rosary to the people she could. Mary said she would have angels to help her teach the rest of the world.

Marie Claire taught the rosary to many people. She always told them that Mother Mary said that this rosary was not to replace the traditional rosary. We should pray it in addition to the traditional rosary. We can pray it every day if we want, as many times as we want. Mary said we should pray it especially on Tuesdays, the day She first gave it to Marie Claire and Fridays, the day Her Son died.

As the Mother of God, Mary had many sorrows in Her life. This rosary is called the Seven Sorrows Rosary. It remembers the seven biggest sorrows Mary suffered. This is what it looks like and how you pray it.

Look closely at the rosary. See how it is different than the traditional rosary. Instead of five sections, there are seven sections (one for each of Mary's biggest sorrows.) Each section has one big bead or medal and seven smaller beads instead of ten like the traditional rosary. Do you see the other difference? Where the traditional rosary has a crucifix, the Seven Sorrows Rosary has a large medal.

Let's learn how to pray it.
We start with the one large bead or medal. There we make the Sign of the Cross. We tell God we want to honor His Holy Mother and think about Her suffering. We ask for graces from our prayers. We pray an Act of Contrition (saying we are sorry for our sins,) and pray a Hail Mary on each of the next three smaller beads

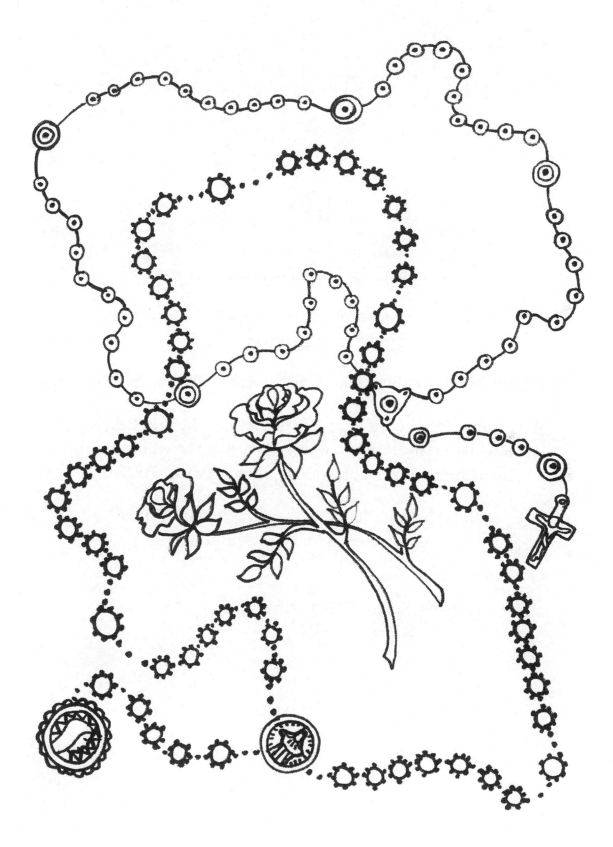

We come to the first set of beads and pray:

"Most merciful Mother remind us always about
the sorrows of Your Son, Jesus."

On these beads we think about Mary's first sorrow: "The Prophecy of Simeon."

Mary brings Jesus to the temple to be blessed. The priest, Simeon,
knows He is God. Simeon warns Mary that She will be hurt
many times because bad things will happen to Her Son.

While we think about that, we pray an Our Father
and seven Hail Marys on the beads.

We come to the second set of beads and pray:

"Most merciful Mother, remind us always about
the sorrows of Your Son, Jesus."

On these beads we think about Mary's second sorrow: "The Flight into Egypt."

Mary's husband, Joseph, woke Her in the middle of the night. He told Her an
angel came to him and said they must leave right away on a long, hard journey.
The angel said a bad king wanted to kill their baby, Jesus. They left right away.
Even though the trip was hard, Mary knew God would keep them safe.

While we think about that, we pray an Our Father
and seven Hail Marys on the beads.

We come to the third set of beads and pray:

"Most merciful Mother, remind us always about
the sorrows of Your Son, Jesus."

On these beads we think about Mary's third sorrow:
"The Loss of Jesus in the Temple."

Like many other people, Mary and Joseph had business in Jerusalem, but it was time to go home. They were traveling with many of their relatives. Mary and Joseph noticed that Jesus wasn't with them. They thought He was with a relative. He wasn't. They searched and searched. For three days they looked, but they couldn't find Him. Mary's heart was breaking. They went back to Jerusalem and finally found Him in the temple talking about holy things. He returned home with them.

While we think about that we pray an Our Father
and seven Hail Marys on the beads.

We come to the fourth set of beads and pray:

"Most merciful Mother, remind us always about
the sorrows of Your Son, Jesus."

On these beads we think of Mary's fourth sorrow:
"Mary Meets Jesus on the Way to Calvary."

Mary met Her Son, Jesus, carrying His cross on the way to Calvary
to die. She saw Him covered in blood from all the beatings He
had been given. She watched as the soldiers pushed Him to hurry
and pulled His hair to force Him to get up when He fell. Every
pain He felt, She felt. Her Mother's heart was broken.

While we think about that we pray an Our Father
and seven Hail Marys on the beads.

We come to the fifth set of beads and pray:

"Most merciful Mother, remind us always of the sorrows of Your Son, Jesus."

On these beads we think about Mary's fifth sorrow:
"Mary Stands at the Foot of the Cross."

Mary followed Her Son, Jesus, to the top of Calvary. She watched as the soldiers stripped Him of His clothes. She saw them nail Him to the cross. Mary's heart ached as Jesus hung painfully on the cross for three hours. When Jesus died, Mary remained standing at the foot of His cross.

While we think about that we pray an Our Father
and seven Hail Marys on the beads.

We come to the sixth set of beads and pray:

"Most merciful Mother, remind us always about
the sorrows of Your Son, Jesus."

On these beads we think of Mary's sixth sorrow:
"Mary Receives the Dead Body of Jesus."

The friends of Jesus, Joseph and Nicodemus took the body of Jesus down
from the cross. They placed it in the outstretched arms of His Mother, Mary.
Even though Her heart was breaking, She gently washed His damaged body.
The worst person in the world had never been treated as badly as Mary's Son.
Still Mary prayed all people would spend eternity with Her Son in heaven.

We think about that when we pray an Our Father
and seven Hail Marys on the beads.

We come to the last set of beads, the seventh set of beads and pray:

"Most merciful Mother, remind us always of the sorrows of Your Son, Jesus."

Mary, John, and the Holy Women placed the body of Jesus in the
tomb. Mary had never felt so alone. She knew Jesus would rise
from the dead, but now all She felt was pain. As we pray we take
up our crosses and add all our sufferings to those of our Mother
Mary. She will take them and give them to Her Son, Jesus.

While we think about that we pray an Our Father
and seven Hail Marys on the beads.

We end the rosary with these prayers.

Queen of Martyrs, Your heart suffered so much, I beg you by the merits of the tears You shed in these terrible and sorrowful times, to obtain for me and all the sinners of the world, the grace of complete sincerity and repentance. Amen.

Mary, Who was conceived without sin and suffered for us, pray for us.

Mary, Who was conceived without sin and suffered for us, pray for us.

Mary, Who was conceived without sin and suffered for us, pray for us.

In the name of the Father, Son, and Holy Spirit. Amen.

Now that you know how to pray the Rosary of the Seven Sorrows, you can pray it whenever you want. You can be one of Mary's angels and help spread it around the world.

Having grown up in a very devout Catholic family in a time when churches were adorned with statues and paintings, Betty was dedicated to the Blessed Virgin, the mother of Christ. After that, she received sixteen years of Catholic education. Today, she works with Rwandan genocide survivor, author, and international speaker, Immaculee Ilibagiza, promoting love, forgiveness and the saying of the Seven Sorrows Rosary. When not traveling, Betty resides in Canon City, Colorado, with her husband, Mike, and their two indoor cats and three outdoor cats.